FIRST STEPS

Pencil Fun 1

S. Cassin & D. Smith

Illustrated by A. Rodger

Collins: Glasgow and London

© 1980 C.E.M.A.
0 00 197009 7
This impression 1986
Printed in Great Britain

All rights reserved. No part of this publication may be reproduced, stored in a retrieval system, or transmitted, in any form or by any means, electronic, mechanical, photocopying, recording or otherwise, without prior permission of the copyright owners.

Where are they going?

A page to practise drawing lines and to encourage left to right movement.
1 Talk about the page. Identify the objects. Ask questions, e.g. What are they? Where are they going?
2 Trace the direction left to right — first pointing with a finger.
3 Ask your child to draw in the lines and colour the page.

Where are they going?

Another page to practise drawing lines and left to right movement.
Talk about the page and identify the objects. Ask questions.
Trace the direction left to right, with a finger first.
Draw in the lines and colour the page.

Where are they going?

More difficult lines to draw and reinforcement of left to right movement.
1 Talk about the page and identify the objects. Ask questions.
2 Trace the direction left to right, with a finger first.
3 Draw in the lines and colour the page.

Shapes to colour

A page designed to practise pencil control and to learn some basic shapes.

Talk about the page. Name the shapes and ask questions about them.

Colour the shapes. Encourage your child to work carefully and to keep within the outlines.

Further activities: Draw round other objects, e.g. saucers, egg cups, boxes, and colour them. Make your own pictures using shapes.

Shapes to colour

More practice in pencil control and learning shapes.

1 Talk about the page. Name some of the shapes.

2 Colour the shapes.

Further activities: Draw round other shapes and colour them. Make pictures using shapes.

Find the way

The first maze. These are designed to encourage a child to think before doing the work.
1 Talk about the page. Encourage conversation about the objects illustrated.
2 Find a way through the maze – first by pointing with a finger.
3 Draw in the line, then colour and decorate the page.

Find the way

Another maze to encourage thinking before doing.
1 Talk about the page.
2 Find a way through the maze — first by pointing with a finger.
3 Draw in the line, then colour and decorate the page.

My house

A page to practise pencil control and to encourage observation.

1 Talk about the page. Identify the parts of the house. Ask questions, e.g. What colour are our curtains? What number is on our door?

2 Draw and colour the curtains. Put some flowers in a vase in one window. Put a number on the door.

Match the shapes

A page to practise recognition of shapes by matching like pairs.
1 Talk about the page. Identify the shapes.
2 Point with a finger to show which two shapes match. One example is given.
3 Join each pair with a line. Colour the shapes.

Match the toys

A page to practise recognition of objects by matching similar toys.
1 Talk about the page. Identify each toy.
2 Point with a finger to similar toys, then join them with a line.
3 Colour the pictures.
Further activities: Find pairs of similar toys. Use string or wool to join them together.

People and hats

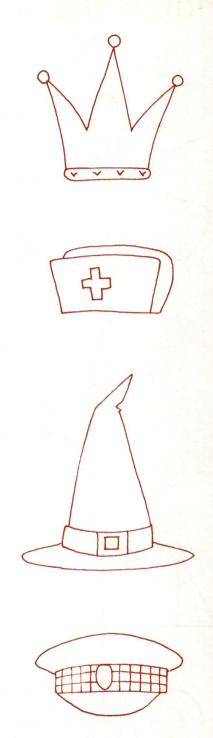

A page to encourage conversation, improve and extend vocabulary and to check general knowledge.

1 Talk about the page. Ask questions about the people.

2 Give the people the correct hat, first by pointing with a finger, then by drawing in lines.

3 Colour the pictures.

Further activities: Make a scrapbook of pictures from magazines/newspapers of people wearing hats.

Follow the prints

A page to practise pencil control and left to right movement.
1 Talk about the page. Ask questions, e.g. Where have they come from? Why? Where are they going now?
2 Follow the prints from left to right with a finger.
3 Draw in direction lines from left to right and colour the pictures.
Further activities: Stand on newspaper, draw round feet and colour the footprints.

Long lines

More practice in pencil control and observation.

1 Talk about the page.
2 Follow the lines with a finger first.
3 Go over the lines with crayon, using a different colour for each line, to show which goes where.

Make them both the same

A page to practise observation and to encourage a child to look carefully at objects.

1 Talk about the page and identify the objects. Ask questions about each pair of objects, e.g. What is different? Why is it different?
2 Make each pair the same by drawing in the missing parts.
3 Colour the pictures.

Which is different?

Another page to give practice in observation.
1 Talk about the page, dealing with one line at a time. Ask questions, e.g. Which is different? Why is it different?
2 Draw a ring round the one object on each line which is different.
3 Colour the pictures.

The tortoise

16

More difficult shapes to colour. Recognition of the colours green, yellow and brown.
1 Talk about the page. Identify and talk about the tortoise.
2 Colour the shapes at the top of the page first, using green, yellow and brown.
3 Colour the tortoise.
Further activities: Use these shapes to make another picture, e.g. an umbrella.

Where are they going?

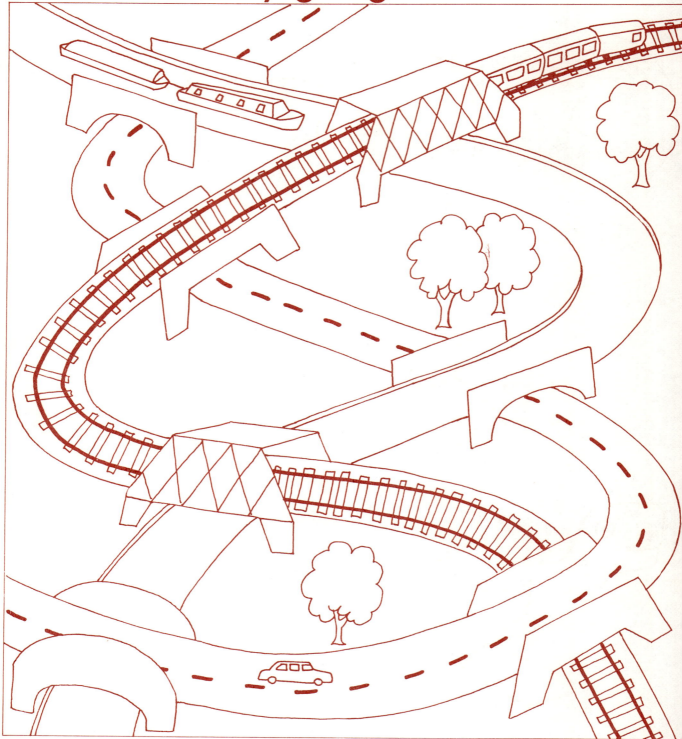

More practice in observation and pencil control.

1 Talk about the page. Identify and ask questions about each object.
2 Show where the boat, train and car are going — first with a finger, then by drawing lines.
3 Colour the picture.

Further activities: Use a toy car, boat or train to show the way. Talk about ways of travelling.

Which way do you go?

More practice in observation and understanding.
Talk about the page. Identify each object.
Point the way with a finger from, for example, home to hospital, station to school. Then draw in routes.
Further activities: Make your own map showing your house and a few local landmarks. Talk about the routes you take to different places.

Odd one out

A page to test observation and understanding of groups of objects. Recognition of the colour blue.
1 Talk about each line in turn. Identify the objects. Ask questions, e.g. Which is the odd one out? Why is it odd?
2 Colour the odd one in each line blue.
Further activities: Collect groups of four objects, three with similarities and one which does not belong to the group.

What is missing?

More practice in observation.
1 Talk about the page. Identify each pair of objects.
2 What is missing? Make each pair the same by drawing in the missing parts.
3 Colour the pictures.

What comes next?

A page to give practice in sequencing by completing a pattern.

1. Talk about each line in turn.
2. Complete each pattern.
3. Colour the patterns.

Further activities: Draw round objects to make up your own patterns.

Patterns

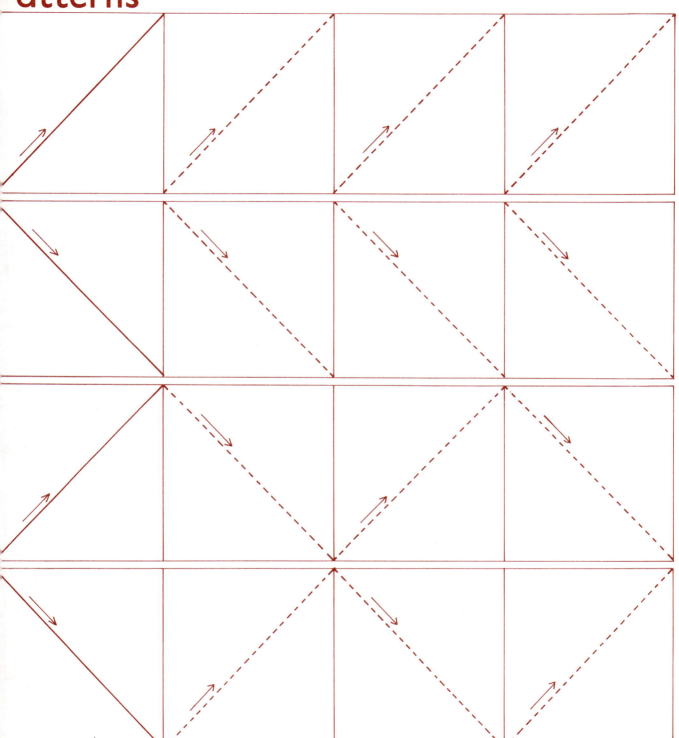

More difficult patterns.
1. Talk about each pattern in turn.
2. Follow the lines with a finger first, then complete the lines. Do one pattern at a time.
3. Colour the patterns.

Further activities: Make more patterns with paint on newspaper.

Follow the dots

Practice in pencil control.
1 Talk about the page.
2 Follow the lines with a finger first, then complete the pictures.
3 Colour the pictures.

Shapes

Observation and knowledge of shapes. Recognition of the colour red.

1 Talk about each line in turn. Identify the shapes.
2 Colour the like shapes on each line red.
3 Colour the other shapes differently.

Odd one out

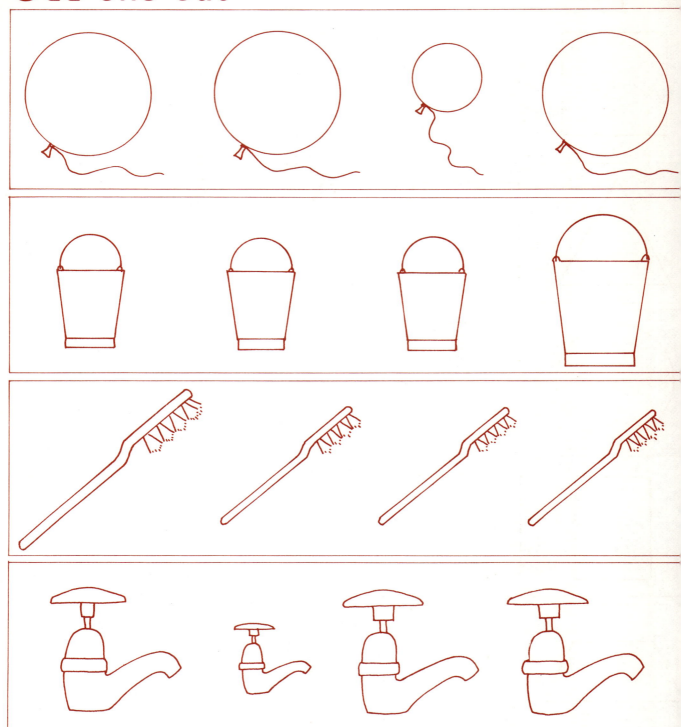

A page to test observation. Recognition of the colour green.
1 Talk about the page. Notice the size of the objects. Ask which is the odd one on each line. Why?
2 Colour the odd ones green.
3 Colour the others differently.
Further activities: Find and draw some big things and some little things.

More patterns

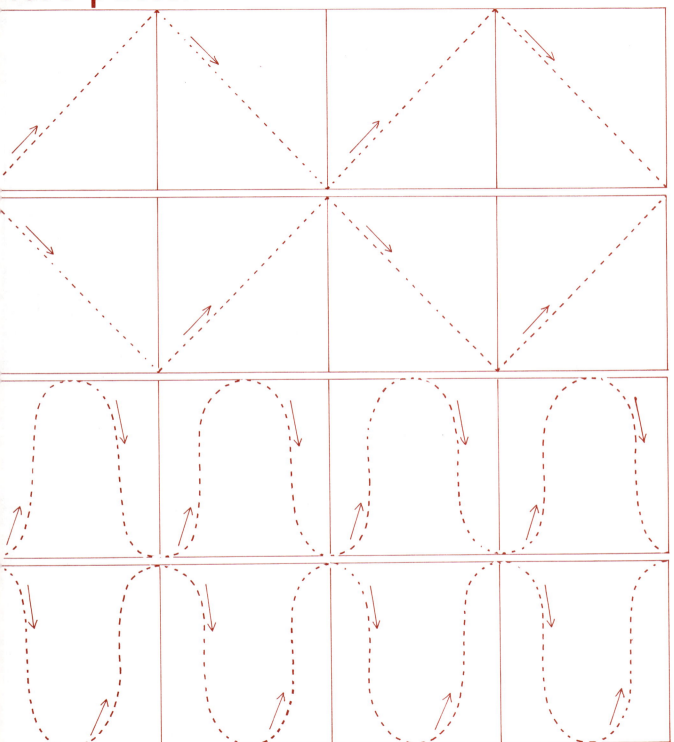

More advanced practice in drawing patterns.
Talk about each pattern in turn.
Follow the lines with a finger first, then complete the patterns.
Colour the patterns.
Further activities: Draw and colour more patterns on newspaper.

Fancy fish

More advanced pencil control is required to complete this page. Recognition of the colours blue and orange.
1 Talk about the page. Talk about fish.
2 Colour the fish blue and orange.
Further activities: Draw and colour more fish of your own.

What comes next?

Completing patterns – sequencing.
- Talk about each line on the page, identifying the objects.
- Complete each pattern.
- Colour the pictures.

Join the dots

More advanced practice in pencil control.

1 Talk about the page. Ask questions, e.g. Where does the tiger live? Where do camels live? What colour are they?
2 Complete the pictures by drawing over the lines.
3 Colour the pictures.

More shapes

☐ red ○ blue △ green ▭ yellow

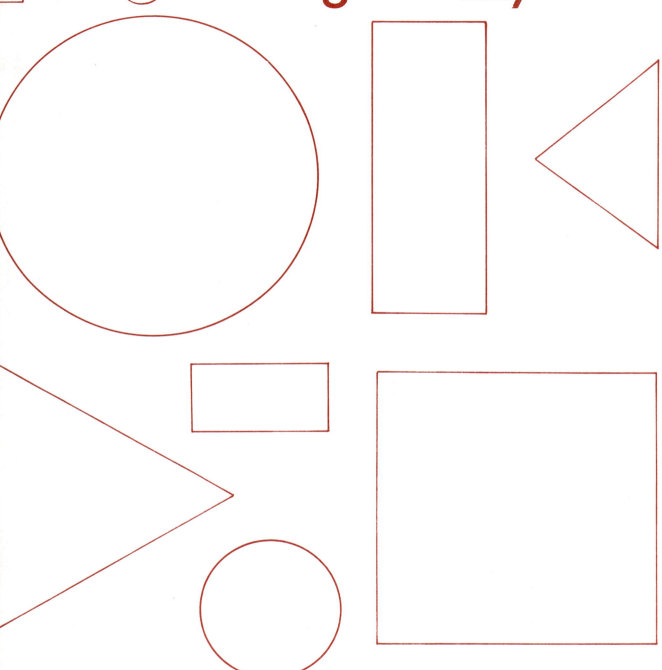

More practice in identifying shapes and following simple instructions. Recognition of the colours red, blue, green and yellow.

Talk about the page. Identify the shapes and colours.

Colour the shapes as instructed.

Further activities: Relate these colours and shapes to life – can you find any in your home?

More shapes

○ yellow ▢ blue △ red ▭ green ⏢ orange

More difficult shapes, following simple instructions.

1 Talk about the page. Name the shapes.
2 Follow instructions and colour the shapes.
Further activities: Make a picture of your own using these shapes.